S0-AEV-782

AMERICAN WAR BIOGRAPHIES

Ulysses S. Grant

E.J. Carter

Heinemann Library
Chicago, Illinois

©2004 Heinemann Library
a division of Reed Elsevier Inc.
Chicago, Illinois

Customer Service 888-454-2279
Visit our website at www.heinemannlibrary.com

All rights reserved. No part of this publication may be reproduced or transmitted in any form or by any means, electronic or mechanical, including photocopying, recording, taping, or any information storage and retrieval system, without permission in writing from the publisher.

Designed by Heinemann Library
Page layout by Lisa Buckley
Maps by John Fleck
Photo research by Janet Lankford Moran
Printed and bound in China by South China Printing
    Company Limited

08 07 06 05 04
10 9 8 7 6 5 4 3 2 1

Library of Congress Cataloging-in-Publication Data
Carter, E. J., 1971-
  Ulysses S. Grant / E.J. Carter.
      p. cm. -- (American war biographies)
Summary: A biography of the Civil War general and United States president who failed at almost everything he tried in his early life, yet went on to achieve significant military, political, and literary accomplishments.
Includes bibliographical references (p.) and index.
  ISBN 1-4034-5080-3 (lib. bdg.) -- ISBN 1-4034-5087-0 (pbk.)
  1. Grant, Ulysses S. (Ulysses Simpson), 1822-1885--Juvenile literature. 2. Presidents--United States--Biography--Juvenile literature. [1. Grant, Ulysses S. (Ulysses Simpson), 1822-1885. 2. Presidents. 3. Generals.] I. Title. II. Series.
  E672.C2925 2004
  973.8'2'092--dc22

                              2003021789

Acknowledgments
The author and publisher are grateful to the following for permission to reproduce photographs:
pp. 5, 20 Medford Historical Society Collection/Corbis; pp. 7l, 25, 37 The Granger Collection, New York; pp. 7r, 10, 18, 23, 30, 41 Corbis; pp. 11, 13, 27, 33, 38, 42 Library of Congress; pp. 15, 28, 35, 43 Bettmann/Corbis

Cover photograph by Library of Congress

The publisher would like to thank Gary Barr for his help in the preparation of this book.

Every effort has been made to contact copyright holders of any material reproduced in this book. Any omissions will be rectified in subsequent printings if notice is given to the publisher.

Some words are shown in bold, **like this.** You can find out what they mean by looking in the glossary.

Contents

Chapter One: Introduction 4

Chapter Two: Lover of Horses 6

Chapter Three: West Point and the Army 8

Chapter Four: Army Life 12

Chapter Five: Making a Living 14

Chapter Six: The Volunteer 17

Chapter Seven: Shiloh 22

Chapter Eight: Vicksburg 26

Chapter Nine: Chattanooga 31

Chapter Ten: General-in-Chief 34

Chapter Eleven: Reconstruction 40

Timeline 44

Further Reading 45

Glossary 46

Index 48

1   Introduction

The nineteenth century was a peaceful period in world history. Few destructive events like the world wars of the twentieth century took place. An exception was the American Civil War (1861–1865), a bitter struggle between northern and southern states over the role of **slavery** and **states' rights** in American society. After the Mexican War of 1846–1848 added new territory to the U.S., debate raged over whether slavery would be extended to those areas, or would remain only in the South. Southerners grew anxious that the North would eventually try to abolish slavery and destroy its way of life. When Abraham Lincoln was elected president in 1860, several states broke away from the **Union** and declared the formation of an independent nation, the **Confederate** States of America. The war that followed was extremely brutal and bloody. After four long years of fighting, the South was defeated and forced back into the Union.

Ulysses S. Grant

Although he began the Civil War as an unknown former soldier who had failed at one job after another, Ulysses S. Grant eventually became the Union's top general. He won major victories at Fort Donelson, Vicksburg, and Chattanooga, before finally defeating Robert E. Lee's army and accepting his surrender at Appomattox Court House. Grant was the only Union general forceful enough to satisfy President Abraham Lincoln. Grant was a tough and ruthless general, throwing wave after wave of Union troops against Confederate defenses. Many of his attacks failed and led to the senseless death of thousands of young troops. But Grant was also a **humane** man. He was opposed to slavery and **racism,** and he cared deeply about his troops. After the war he tried his best to create harmony between blacks and whites and between North and South.

Ulysses S. Grant led his troops with energy and determination. He also had the ability to learn from past experiences. These traits helped Grant in both his military and political careers.

After the Civil War ended, Grant was the most popular person in the United States. He was easily elected president in 1868 and again in 1872. Although his two terms in office were not very successful, he remained the most important political figure of the postwar era. Before Grant died in 1885, the famous writer Mark Twain convinced him to write his **memoirs.** The result was one of the best autobiographies by any American. Grant's career is an inspiring story of a man who failed at almost everything he tried in his early life, yet went on to record incredible military, political, and literary accomplishments.

2 Lover of Horses

1821

June 24
Jesse Grant and
Hannah Simpson
married in Ohio

1822

April 27
Ulysses Grant born
in Point Pleasant,
Ohio

1823

Grant family
moved to
Georgetown

1836

Ulysses attended
preparatory school
in Maysville

1837

Jesse Grant
elected mayor
of Georgetown

Grant was born in 1822 in Point Pleasant, Ohio, about twenty miles from Cincinnati. His full name was Hiram Ulysses Grant, but everyone called him Ulysses. Even though his parents, Jesse and Hannah Grant, had received little schooling, they were well-educated for that time and place. They loved to read and were interested in politics. Jesse Grant was a **tanner.** He made leather from the hides of cattle.

The year after Ulysses was born, the family moved to Georgetown, Ohio. Jesse and Hannah opened their own tannery, bought a brick home, and had five more children. Jesse expanded his business, selling leather goods and supplies. He got involved in local politics. Later, in 1837, he would be elected mayor of Georgetown. Jesse was fiercely opposed to the practice of **slavery.** He claimed that he had moved from Kentucky to Ohio as a young man because he did not want to live in a slave state. Throughout his life he supported the **abolitionist** cause.

Abolitionists and slavery

Abolitionists were people opposed to slavery and the slave trade. In both Europe and the United States they formed societies, led **boycotts** and protests, and supported political candidates who represented their cause. Some of them operated the "Underground Railroad," which transported runaway slaves to freedom. In the U.S. the best-known abolitionist was William Lloyd Garrison, who created the American Anti-Slavery Society in 1833. Other prominent abolitionists included ministers like Theodore Dwight Weld and Theodore Parker and former slaves such as Frederick Douglass and William Wells Brown. The abolitionist community was also inspired by Harriet Beecher Stowe's novel, *Uncle Tom's Cabin* (1852).

6

Above: Grant was born in this house in Point Pleasant, Ohio, in 1822.
Right: This photograph shows Ulysses S. Grant's parents, Hanna Simpson and Jesse Root Grant.

As a boy Ulysses worked in his father's tannery, but he did not want to follow in Jesse's footsteps. He did not like the tanning business and wanted to avoid it. He hated the smell of the soaking and drying skins. His parents found that he was much more interested in living animals, especially horses. Ulysses had a strong attachment to horses from the time he was very young. By the age of five he could ride a horse while standing on its back. His friends and neighbors were especially amazed at his ability to tame wild horses.

Education

When he grew older Ulysses still refused to become a tanner. His father decided to send him to the United States Military Academy in **West Point,** New York. Ulysses was good at math and after a year at a preparatory school in Maysville, his scores were high enough to earn admission. Jesse used his political connections to secure a spot for his son. But the townspeople of Georgetown believed Grant would only be an average **cadet.** They suspected that he was destined to be a failure.

3 West Point and the Army

1839–1843

Grant attended the
United States
Military Academy

1843

September
Grant reports to
Jefferson Barracks
near St. Louis

1844

April
Grant and Julia
Dent become
engaged to be
married

April
Grant sent to
Camp Salubrity
in Louisiana

1845

September
Grant sent to
Corpus Christi,
Texas

1846

May 8
First battle of
the Mexican
War begins

To some degree the townspeople were right. Grant worked hard at **West Point** and continued to do well in mathematics. But his marks in French and other subjects were poor. He graduated in 1843 in the bottom half of his class (21st out of 39). Grant spent a lot of time in the library reading adventure novels by James Fenimore Cooper and Washington Irving. He also developed a passion for painting and drawing, and one of his pictures still hangs in the United States Military Academy. The most common subject of his paintings were horses. Meanwhile, he continued to amaze his fellow students with his ability to ride and tame wild horses.

This map shows the many places Grant traveled to in his early military career.

Grant also acquired his name at West Point. When he arrived in New York someone had mistakenly recorded his name as Ulysses S. Grant instead of Ulysses H. Grant. From that time forward he would be known as U.S. Grant. Some of his classmates nicknamed him "Uncle Sam." This patriotic-sounding name would boost Grant's popularity and help spread his fame during the Civil War.

Some soldiers who would later become famous generals and Civil War figures attended West Point at the same time as Grant. William T. Sherman, George H. Thomas, George B. Mc Clellan, and Thomas J. Jackson were major participants in the Civil War. But Grant did not attract the attention of these **elite** young men. He stood just over 5 feet (1.5 meters) tall when he started at West Point. He was also not a great student and did not come from an important family. Grant spent most of his time alone, or with a small group of friends that included Frederick Dent, Rufus Ingalls, and Simon Bolivar Buckner—none of whom would later become famous soldiers.

After graduation Grant had a four-year commitment to serve in the army. He did not plan to pursue a military career after that. After his discharge, he hoped to find a position as a professor of mathematics. Given his love of horses, he hoped to be assigned to the **cavalry,** but instead he was sent to join the Fourth **Infantry** in Missouri.

First assignment

Grant was sent to Jefferson Barracks outside St. Louis as part of his first army assignment. Many famous soldiers were stationed at this military post at least once during their careers. Grant's good friend Frederick Dent was also assigned to St. Louis, which pleased them both. Dent's family lived nearby on a large **plantation** named White Haven. Grant spent a lot of time at his friend's estate whenever he could get time away from the barracks. Dent had several younger sisters and soon Grant was coming to the Dent plantation even more frequently than before. He had fallen in love with the eldest daughter, Julia Dent.

By April 1844 they were engaged to be married. Julia kept the engagement secret from her father, who did not want his daughter to marry an army officer. She also believed that at nineteen she was too young to get married. They did not have much time to plan their next move. Grant was reassigned to Camp Salubrity, near Natchitoches, Louisiana. She accepted his class ring, having no idea that it would be four long years before they would be married. A year later, Grant returned to St. Louis to see Julia. He asked her father for permission to marry her, but her father refused.

At War in Mexico

Grant again followed his army unit to a new location, this time in Corpus Christi, Texas. The United States was inching toward war with Mexico. President James K. Polk posted troops, including Grant's unit, on the Mexican border, hoping to start a conflict over Texas. Grant would later call the Mexican War "one of the most unjust

Julia Dent Grant was the sister of one of Grant's **West Point** classmates. After their engagement, the threat of war with Mexico delayed their wedding.

ever waged by a stronger against a weaker nation." He believed that the real issue behind the conflict was the desire among Southerners to add more slave states to the **Union.**

Despite his doubts, Grant served bravely under General Zachary Taylor in early battles at Matamoros, Monterey, and Buena Vista. Grant was made **quartermaster** of the Fourth Infantry. His job was to get wagons loaded with supplies and soldiers to the right place at the right time. He would have preferred to join a combat unit, but he soon found his work as quartermaster was both important and dangerous. His units came under fire frequently and he quickly realized how important a good quartermaster was to the success of an army. This was knowledge that would prove useful when he became a general himself.

In January 1847 Grant was transferred to General Winfield Scott's army. Zachary Taylor was not liked by President Polk, and Scott was picked to command the final invasion of Mexico. Grant again served with great skill and bravery in the battles of

Vera Cruz and Mexico City. At the gates of the capital city, Grant rushed a group of men and a small cannon into a church tower. From this location he was able to rain fire down on the defenders. His act was so helpful to the American victory that he was mentioned in the news reports sent to Washington, D.C. The Mexican general, Santa Anna, surrendered, and the war was over. In the months that followed, Grant hiked through the Mexican countryside, learned a little Spanish, and developed a strong attachment to the country. He continued, though, to feel guilty about the American invasion.

Quartermasters

The term quartermaster means "master of quarters [rooms]." It was first used when full-time armies were created in the 16th and 17th centuries. The quartermaster was the person who provided lodging and supplies for troops. The first American Quartermaster Corps dates from 1775. The Second Continental Congress created the position of Quartermaster General and gave the job to General Thomas Mifflin. But the "father of the Quartermaster Corps" was Thomas Sidney Jesup, who ran the Quartermaster Department from 1818 to 1860. He improved methods of transporting soldiers and supplied them with clothing, as well as food, lodging, and weapons.

At the Battle of Monterrey during the Mexican War, Grant volunteered to carry a message through a street lined with enemy snipers.

4 Army Life

1848

August 22
Grant and Julia
Dent married

1850

May
Frederick, their
first son, born

1852

July 5
Grant left New
York for San
Francisco, then
Fort Vancouver

1854

January 5
Grant reassigned
to Fort Humboldt,
California

April 11
Grant resigned
from the army

Toward the end of the war, Grant learned that Julia Dent's father had dropped his objections to their marriage. In July 1848 he was finally able to return to St. Louis. He and Julia were married on August 22. After visiting Grant's relatives in Ohio and Kentucky, the couple moved to Detroit, Michigan, where the **quartermaster** was now assigned.

For Julia the transition to army life was difficult. She missed her father and her family, and she had to learn to live without the slaves who used to take care of her. She frequently returned to St. Louis on long visits. In May 1850 she gave birth to their first child, Frederick Dent Grant.

Trekking across Panama

In 1852 the army again asked Grant to move, this time to the California. To get there his unit would have to travel all the way to Panama, cross over to the Pacific Ocean, then travel back up to San Francisco. Grant was extremely disappointed at this news. His wife was expecting another baby and would not be able to travel with him. He would be alone for many months, if not years. Grant was a loving father and he worried his children would forget him in his absence.

The journey was very difficult. After reaching Central America by ship, the army had to march across Panama to the Pacific Ocean. There they boarded another ship for California. Almost all of Grant's men fell ill from **cholera** and other diseases and one-third of them died. Grant helped nurse the sick men back to health while trying to make sure the unit's supplies safely reached their destination.

Lonely in Oregon and California

Finally the expedition reached San Francisco. Grant was sent to Fort Vancouver in Oregon and then to Fort Humboldt in California. He was miserable. He missed his family terribly and he did not enjoy his work. His health began to suffer and the wet winters bothered him. He rarely received letters from Julia. Either she did not write often or her letters were lost in the long journey across the continent.

Soon his fellow officers noticed that Grant had begun drinking, sometimes heavily. He drank partly because he was lonely and depressed and partly because of his poor health. Rumors began to spread that Grant was an alcoholic, but it is hard to know how much of this is true. Later his enemies would use stories of his drinking to **discredit** his performance during the Civil War.

Finally Grant could not take it any longer. In April 1854 he received a promotion to captain and on the same day he **resigned** from the army. He began the journey across the western United States. At long last he would be reunited with his family.

Fort Vancouver in the Oregon Territory was a lonely place. Grant did not bring his family to this post because his army wages would not support them. While Grant was at Fort Vancouver, his wife and son lived with Grant's parents in Ohio.

5 Making a Living

1855

August
Grant arrives back
in St. Louis and
begins farming

1856

Summer
Hardscrabble built

1860

April
Grant family arrives
in Galena, Illinois,
to take over family
general store

November
Abraham Lincoln
elected president

1860–1861

December 1860–
March 1861
Seven Southern
states **secede** from
the **Union** and form
the Confederate
States of America

1861

March 13
American Civil
War begins at
Fort Sumter

Grant arrived at the Dent **plantation** in August, and he finally met his second son, Ulysses Jr., for the first time. Now that he had left the army, Grant needed to find a new job. He decided to go into farming. Julia's father had given her 60 acres (24 hectares) of land as a wedding present. With help from the Dent slaves, Grant planted wheat, corn, and potatoes on the land. The crops were large, but prices were low. To gain extra income, Grant hauled firewood into St. Louis and sold it on cold street corners.

Grant's views on slavery

Grant was uncomfortable with the practice of **slavery.** He opposed it, but perhaps not as fiercely as his father, who continued to support the **abolitionist** movement in Ohio. Grant worked alongside slaves and treated them well. But Grant's family ties to the slave-owning Dents prevented him from speaking out strongly against slavery. Julia herself owned four house servants. Grant wanted to set them free, but he could not force his wife to do that.

During their farming years, the Grants lived in a house owned by Julia's father, but in 1855, Ulysses decided to build his own home. He constructed a small log cabin and named it "Hardscrabble." He was confident about his new occupation. In 1856 he wrote to his father, "Every day I like farming better and I do not doubt but that money is to be made at it."

Real estate

But by early 1858, Grant's farming operation was in trouble. He had fallen into debt and exhausted himself through hard work. Meanwhile Julia had given birth to two more children, and his income could not feed a family of six. He decided to try a new job. A relative of the Dents had a real estate business in St. Louis and he accepted Grant as his partner. This job did not last long; Grant was not good at business matters and there was not enough money to share between the two partners.

Finally in 1859 Grant turned to his father for help. The family owned a general store in Galena, Illinois. Jesse's brother Simpson was in poor health, and Ulysses was allowed to manage the store. In the summer of 1860, the family packed up its belongings and headed up the Mississippi River. Grant hated the paperwork associated with running the business. However, he hoped that there, out of the shadow of his wealthy father-in-law, he could make a new start.

In 1855, Grant built a cabin he named "Hardscrabble" near St. Louis, Missouri. He and his family lived there until 1860, when they moved to Galena, Illinois.

Approach of the Civil War

Grant had been too busy trying to feed his family over the past several years to pay too much attention to politics. He opposed **slavery**, but not enough to support the new **Republican Party.** He feared that it would create division within the country. In 1856 he voted for James Buchanan, a member of the **Democratic Party,** for president. In St. Louis he listened to many discussions of **secession** among those who supported slavery. When Abraham Lincoln was elected president in 1860, he knew the South might carry out its threat to **secede.** That is exactly what happened. In December 1860 and January 1861, six southern states formed the **Confederate** States of America and declared their independence from the Union. Over the next few months, five more states (Texas, Arkansas, Tennessee, Virginia, and North Carolina) would join the cause as well.

Harper's Ferry

An important event leading to the Civil War was John Brown's raid on Harper's Ferry. Brown was a passionate **abolitionist** who was willing to use violence to achieve his aims. Earlier he had killed three defenders of slavery in Kansas, but he was never captured. He began planning to build a colony for runaway slaves. He needed supplies and weapons, so on October 16, 1859, he attacked a federal **arsenal** at Harper's Ferry, Virginia. He hoped this might inspire a slave rebellion. Instead, gunfire broke out and several people were killed. The U.S. government sent Robert E. Lee, soon to become the Confederacy's most famous general, to end the uprising. On October 18 Brown's raiders were captured, and Brown was executed on December 2. The South was deeply shaken by John Brown's raid, and it helped convince many that Republicans and abolitionists might succeed in abolishing slavery. To prevent this, they seceded when Lincoln was elected.

In April 1861 Grant listened to a speech outside the Galena courthouse. The first shots of the Civil War had been fired at Fort Sumter, South Carolina, days earlier. In response, Lincoln called for 75,000 volunteers to serve in state **militias.** A man named John A. Rawlins spoke that day. He was a Democrat but he called for political differences to be set aside. "There can be but two parties now, one of patriots and one of traitors!" he argued. The speech had a powerful effect on Grant, who was the only person in Galena with professional military training. He decided to join the army once again.

6 The Volunteer

Grant hoped to win a position as a **colonel** in the Illinois militia. He traveled to Springfield, the state capital, and filed a **petition** with Governor Richard Yates. Yates did not appoint him to a post right away, but invited him to help organize the Illinois volunteers. This meant more paperwork, which Grant did not enjoy. But by May he had begun drilling and training new **recruits** in the southern Illinois region. He impressed many of the men with his ability, and finally on June 15, 1861, Yates named Grant colonel of the Seventh District **Regiment.**

Taming the troops

Grant's men in Springfield were extremely undisciplined. They had not respected their previous colonel, and they broke army rules frequently. Grant quickly brought order to the regiment. He was as skilled at taming unruly men as he was at taming wild horses.

Soon the troops, now known as the Twenty-First Illinois, were ready for their first action. They were sent to Missouri, a state that was deeply divided between **loyalists** and **secessionists.** Small groups of secessionist soldiers were trying to force Missouri to join the **Confederacy,** and Grant's troops were sent to fight them. The Northerners could not be too aggressive, though, since that might swing the state's **sympathies** toward the South.

Grant never found the raiders he was looking for, but the discipline shown by his troops as they marched through Missouri won him great praise. Grant was asked to bring order to other regiments stationed in Missouri.

1861

June 15
Grant named colonel of the Seventh District Regiment

August
Grant promoted to **Brigadier General** of Volunteers

September 6
Grant's army takes Paducah, Kentucky

November 7
Attack on Belmont, Missouri

1862

February 5–15
Forts Henry, Donelson, and Heiman taken

After the Civil War began in 1861, President Lincoln asked for army volunteers. The governor of Illinois, Richard Yates, appointed Grant **colonel** of a regiment that became known as the 21st Illinois Volunteers.

In August Grant was promoted to **brigadier general** of volunteers. He was enjoying more success than at any other time of his career. But he still had not seen much action. He and his troops were in Ironton in the Ozark Mountains when the **Union** was defeated at the Battle of Wilson's Creek. This was the North's second major loss of the war. In July Union troops had been defeated at the Battle of Bull Run/Manassas in Virginia.

First battle

Grant did not have much time to enjoy his promotion. In September he was sent to Cairo, Illinois, as the Union prepared to battle for Kentucky. Grant entered the town of Paducah and promised the citizens that as long as they did not rebel against the U.S., they and their property would be left alone. Kentucky, like Missouri, was a **neutral** state, and this policy helped prevent the state from **seceding.**

Julia and his children joined him in Cairo. They would frequently visit his army camps at different spots around the country. It was not common for women to spend so much time in the midst of war scenes. But Julia Grant was a very strong woman and she did not mind the hardships of travel and camp life. Grant's life was much easier when he was with her and his children.

On November 7 Grant learned that **Confederate** troops had set up camp at Belmont, on the Missouri side of the Mississippi River. Finally he would see his first real fighting of the Civil War. He led five **regiments** down the river by steamboat, and early in the morning they attacked. Grant thought his force was too small to do any real damage, but to his surprise the Confederate troops fled and he captured 100 soldiers. Grant's men began celebrating their victory.

The Confederates had three forts controlling important locations on the Tennessee and Cumberland Rivers.

"Old Brains"

Henry Halleck graduated from **West Point** in 1839. He served in the U.S. Army, fought in the Mexican War, and later taught at West Point. He wrote several books on military affairs and picked up the nickname "Old Brains." In 1854 he moved to San Francisco and practiced law. He helped draft the California state constitution. When the Civil War began he was awarded a series of high positions, including general-in-chief. He was an excellent administrator, but among the public he was extremely unpopular. He remained in the army after the war and died in Kentucky in 1872.

But they celebrated too soon. The **Confederates,** led by Gideon Pillow and Leonidas Polk, regrouped and attacked. Grant had to retreat quickly. He piled his men into the transport ships and steamed back to Cairo. Grant was courageous in battle, but he sometimes **underestimated** his opponent. He was completely unprepared for Pillow and Polk's counterattack.

Into Tennessee

That winter Grant prepared to send his army further south. The Tennessee and Cumberland Rivers were perfect targets, offering a path deep into the Confederacy. The Confederates had built three forts—Fort Donelson, Fort Henry, and Fort Heiman—to protect these rivers from invasion. If he could capture these forts, Grant would control all of western Tennessee. Finally in late January he received permission to attack from his commander, General Henry Halleck.

Fort Heiman would not be a problem because it was still under construction. Grant planned to cut off the road between Forts Donelson and Henry so they could not combine their forces. But instead the Confederates left Fort Henry before Grant even arrived. He would have to mount a major assault against Fort Donelson. On February 14 Grant was ready. He hoped that navy gunboats commanded by Andrew H. Foote could do most of the fighting. But on the first day of the battle, Fort Donelson's guns battered Foote's fleet. The ships had to return to Cairo to be repaired. While Foote and Grant discussed the situation, the Confederates mounted a surprise attack and drove back the **Union's** right **flank.**

Grant could have panicked, but he kept his cool and ordered a counterattack on the left flank. Charles F. Smith's troops broke through the Confederate lines and by the following morning Fort Donelson was ready to give up. The victory made Grant a hero in the North. He was promoted to major general. Suddenly newspapers referred to him as "Unconditional Surrender" Grant. Rumors spread that Grant led his troops carrying nothing but a cigar, and this led to the popularity of smoking cigars.

Ghosts of the past

But Grant's victories had a negative side. Some military officers were jealous of his success, or disliked him for various reasons. To ruin his reputation, they claimed that Grant was an alcoholic. Throughout the rest of the war, any time Grant's forces suffered a defeat or setback, his critics would accuse him of drunkenness. In fact, it is unlikely that Grant had a drinking problem during the Civil War. But he never put his past entirely behind him.

7 Shiloh

1862

March
Halleck given
command in
the West

April 6–7
Battle of
Shiloh/Pittsburg
Landing

May
Beauregard's
evacuation of
Corinth

July 17
Grant took
command of the
District of West
Tennessee

One of Grant's enemies was his commander, Henry Halleck. Halleck tried to take credit for the victories at Fort Henry and Fort Donelson, and when that failed, he tried to get Grant fired. Grant, hoping to take the whole state of Tennessee after his victory, had marched from Fort Donelson to Clarksville, then to Nashville, where he found a large **Confederate** army. Halleck now accused him of not following orders. He also told his superiors in Washington that Grant had begun drinking. Halleck was afraid Grant's success would interfere with his own march up the army ladder. Finally Halleck was given command of all **Union** troops in the West, and his bad feelings toward Grant disappeared. By then, however, Grant had given up his attempt to take Tennessee, which might have led to an earlier end to the war.

Grant's army was now camped at Pittsburg Landing, near the Tennessee-Mississippi border. A large Confederate army led by Sidney Johnston had formed to oppose them. Grant believed the South was in the process of crumbling and prepared to attack. Neither he nor the general supervising the forces, William T. Sherman, expected a Confederate **ambush.** They were completely taken by surprise on the morning of April 6 when Johnston's forces struck the first blow. When Grant arrived at Pittsburg Landing, he found chaos. His men were retreating through the woods. The remaining soldiers gave up ground quickly. General Benjamin Prentiss's troops were caught in marshy ground near a peach orchard. For hours they tried to resist the attack, but the fighting was so fierce that few made it out alive.

Once again Grant refused to panic. Prentiss's troops had bought him some time. He waited for **reinforcements** from William Nelson and Don Carlos Buell. With these extra men he believed he could hold off the Southern advance. Finally toward the end of the day Nelson's troops arrived, while Joseph Webster's gunboats provided badly needed help. Still, if the Confederates had pushed forward that night, they might have destroyed Grant's army.

During the night it began to rain, and more reinforcements arrived, including Buell. The following morning Grant ordered a massive attack against the Confederates. The battle was concentrated near Shiloh Church. By afternoon the Southerners, now led by Pierre Beauregard after Johnston was shot, retreated to Corinth, Mississippi. Three thousand men died in those two days of fighting, more than had died in the entire Revolutionary and Mexican Wars combined. The remaining troops were so exhausted that Grant missed a chance to chase the fleeing Confederates to Corinth. He wrote to Buell, "The great fatigue of our men, they having been engaging in two days fight . . . would preclude an advance tonight."

Above, men in the 1st Ohio **Infantry Regiment** recapture artillery at Shiloh Church, near Pittsburg Landing, on April 7, 1862. During the Battle of Pittsburg Landing, Grant pushed back Southern forces.

A blow to Grant's reputation

The battle of Shiloh had been extremely bloody, far more destructive than anything Grant had seen before. He also had not prepared his troops for the possibility of an attack. Suddenly Grant's good reputation in the north vanished. The general learned that public opinion changed quickly and was often unfair. Many urged Lincoln to dismiss him, but he refused. "I can't spare this man; he fights," the president said. But Lincoln himself was upset by the number of **casualties** suffered at Shiloh.

Halleck again attempted to reorganize the army, removing many of Grant's troops from his direct command. Grant was given the meaningless position of second-in-command in the western theater. Without his own troops, he would have very little authority. On April 30, Halleck himself led the **Union** forces down to Corinth, 20 miles (32 kilometers) south of Pittsburg Landing. Shortly before they arrived, however, Beauregard cleared out his troops. After this bloodless victory, Halleck returned Grant to his old position. Soon Halleck would be promoted to general-in-chief and moved to Washington, D.C. Grant, who had considered **resigning,** went back to work planning the invasion of Mississippi.

During this period, Grant developed a very close relationship with William T. Sherman. Sherman helped keep Grant's spirits up in the aftermath of Shiloh. Sherman had had his own problems earlier in the war, and he urged Grant not to give up.

Bringing order to the countryside

Grant's new headquarters were in Memphis. He now was responsible for all of western Tennessee and northern Mississippi. He spent the next several months trying to bring order to these areas. He hoped he could persuade the local residents to give up the cause of **secession** and transfer their loyalties to the Union. But he was surprised at the strong resistance he encountered. Attacks on his troops and anger toward the Union forces suggested that Tennesseeans were still willing to fight. Grant began to think the war might last longer than he originally believed.

William T. Sherman

A major reason why the Union was not badly defeated at Shiloh was the brilliant leadership shown by one of Grant's generals, William T. Sherman. Sherman was born in Ohio in 1820. His father died when he was young and he was raised by a family friend, Thomas Ewing. He graduated from **West Point** in 1840 and was stationed in San Francisco. In 1853 he resigned from the army to work at a bank. Later he became superintendent of the Louisiana State Seminary and Military Academy. When the Civil War broke out, he returned to the North and joined the **infantry.** He fought in the first major battle of the war at Manassas/Bull Run, where the Union was soundly defeated. Sherman soon was given an important command in Kentucky, but he suffered a nervous breakdown when the press turned against him. But Sherman turned out to be Grant's most reliable advisor and supporter. After the war he became commander of the entire U.S. army before retiring in 1883.

One of the biggest problems he faced was what to do with freed or escaped Southern slaves. Northern cities refused to take in **refugees.** Grant decided to create camps for these black families. They would be employed to work on cotton fields for wages. He hoped this would ease the transition from **slavery** to freedom, while overcoming **racist** attitudes in the North and South alike.

8 Vicksburg

1862

September 19
Price and Van
Dorn's attack on
Corinth

December 29
Sherman defeated
at Chickasaw
Bayou

1863

April 16
Porter's fleet sails
past Vicksburg

April 30
Grant crosses
Mississippi River
at Bruinsberg

May 14
Fall of Jackson

May 16
Battle of
Champion Hill

July 4
Surrender of
Vicksburg

In the summer of 1862, **Confederate** forces went on the offensive. Robert E. Lee invaded Maryland, and two generals named Sterling Price and Earl Van Dorn attempted to take back Corinth. Grant planned the defense of the city while visiting St. Louis. The attack failed, and the Confederates retreated to Holly Springs.

Grant was free to plan his attack on Vicksburg, Mississippi. Vicksburg was the key to controlling the entire Mississippi River. The **Union** had already conquered New Orleans and the mouth of the Mississippi. With Vicksburg they would dominate the main trade route through the western states. In addition, they would have divided the Confederacy into two parts, and it would be almost impossible for the South to defend Texas, Arkansas, and western Louisiana.

First attempt

Grant's campaign began in December 1862. He sent William T. Sherman, his most trusted general, down the Mississippi with 32,000 men. Grant would then push deep into central Mississippi, hoping to distract John C. Pemberton, the defender of Vicksburg. The plan failed. Grant was blocked by Nathan Bedford Forrest's troops and he could not support Sherman. At Chickasaw Bayou, north of Vicksburg, Sherman was soundly defeated.

Grant takes command

Grant decided he would have to lead the invasion himself. A Union general named John A. McClernand had become the second-highest ranking officer in Grant's army. But

John Pemberton graduated from **West Point** in 1837. Though he was born in Pennsylvania, he chose to fight for the Confederacy in 1861. At Vicksburg in 1863, he proved to be no match for Grant.

McClernand owed his position to political connections rather than skill. Grant could not trust him with such an important operation.

Grant tried out several new plans for his attack on Vicksburg. One idea was to dig a canal that would turn the Mississippi River from the city. This would make Vicksburg vulnerable to attack. Grant's men spent a great deal of time digging canals and waterways, but nothing worked. Yet he remained optimistic. "I will have Vicksburg this month or fail in the attempt," he told Halleck.

Finally, Grant settled on his next move. He led his troops down the western side of the Mississippi River and looked for a good spot to cross the river. Meanwhile, in a daring move, Admiral David D. Porter led his fleet of barges, gunboats, and transport ships down the river past the guns of Vicksburg. Porter's ships could easily have been smashed to pieces, but most of them made it through. To confuse Pemberton, Grant also sent Benjamin Grierson into central Mississippi with 500 skilled soldiers. Grierson's job was to tear up railroads and cause as much trouble as possible. This led Pemberton to send part of his army to chase Grierson. While Pemberton was distracted, Grant's troops crossed into Mississippi territory.

Although each of Porter's ships was hit repeatedly by the guns of Vicksburg, only one transport ship was lost the night of April 16, 1863.

The Emancipation Proclamation

Abraham Lincoln's Emancipation Proclamation was issued January 1, 1863. Notice that Lincoln does not declare all slaves free, but only those living in states that have rebelled against the United States:

That on the 1st day of January, A.D. 1863, all persons held as slaves within any State or designated part of a State the people whereof shall then be in rebellion against the United States shall be then, thenceforward, and forever free; and the executive government of the United States, including the military and naval authority thereof, will recognize and maintain the freedom of such persons and will do no act or acts to repress such persons, or any of them, in any efforts they may make for their actual freedom.

Inside Mississippi

Once across the river, the army was met by a **Confederate** force under John S. Bowen near Port Gibson. The battle was close, but the **Union** won. Grierson's raid had weakened the Confederates just enough to allow Grant to triumph.

Southern armies, led by Joseph E. Johnston, raced toward Vicksburg to back up Pemberton, and Grant had to hurry. But Grant's army needed supplies. He decided to let the troops live off the surrounding countryside while he pressed on. His plan was to threaten both Jackson, the state capital, and Vicksburg. That would keep the Confederate armies divided. Sherman and James McPherson conquered Jackson with little trouble on May 14.

The siege of Vicksburg

Meanwhile, Pemberton led his forces out from Vicksburg to Champion Hill, hoping to join up with Joseph E. Johnston's troops. But Union spies **intercepted** a message from Johnston to Pemberton describing this plan. Grant then pounced on Pemberton at Champion Hill. He won a tremendous

Grant led a successful attack against Pemberton's forces during the Battle of Champion Hill on May 16, 1863.

victory and sent the Confederates scurrying back to Vicksburg. By May 19 Grant had surrounded Vicksburg and was ready to attack. But the first two attempts to take the city failed. Grant would have to starve Pemberton out, cutting off his supplies until he gave up. Meanwhile he had to worry about Johnston leading Confederate **reinforcements** to lift the **siege.** But inside Vicksburg, Pemberton's troops were growing hungry and exhausted. On July 4 he surrendered.

Instead of taking the 30,000 men inside prisoner, Grant let them return to their homes, if they promised not to fight anymore. This was the biggest victory of the war for the Union so far. Grant received another promotion. He was now major general in the regular army, and he was placed in charge of the entire area between the Appalachian Mountains and the Mississippi River.

9 Chattanooga

efore undertaking his next move, Grant needed to rest his troops. The conquest of Vicksburg took many months, and the wet, hot conditions meant than the soldiers were frequently ill. To replenish his army's ranks, Grant tried to **recruit** African-American soldiers. Many slaves set free by the January 1, 1863, Emancipation Proclamation were willing to fight in the **Union** army, and Grant took advantage of this: "The negro troops are easier to preserve discipline among than our White troops and I doubt not will prove equally good for **garrison** duty. All that have been tried have fought bravely."

Grant hoped to take his army east to Mobile, Alabama. But Halleck wanted him to conquer Texas, which now was separated from the rest of the **Confederacy** by the Mississippi River. Grant traveled to New Orleans to meet with Nathaniel P. Banks, the general guarding the mouth of the Mississippi. After reviewing troops one afternoon, Grant was thrown off his horse and badly hurt. This incident again sparked rumors about his drinking. People assumed that such an excellent horseman must have been drunk to be thrown off his horse.

Crisis in Tennessee

While Grant was recuperating, Halleck changed his mind about the invasion of Texas. In eastern Tennessee the Union General William Rosecrans was facing a tough fight with Confederate forces led by Braxton Bragg. He was cornered near Chattanooga and needed help. Rosecrans was removed from his post, and Grant took over the operation.

1863

September 4
Grant thrown from his horse and injured

October 5
Halleck asked Grant to come to Chattanooga

October 27–28
Brown's ferry captured

November 15
Sherman arrived in Chattanooga

November 25
Battle of Chattanooga

31

His first task was to feed the troops. The **Union's** Army of the Cumberland was weak and hungry, and Bragg had cut off its supply routes. On October 27 and 28, Grant sent soldiers to capture Brown's Ferry on the Tennessee River. This opened up a path to get food and ammunition to the army.

But the **Confederates** still enjoyed a very strong position. Bragg had placed his troops along Missionary Ridge and on Lookout Mountain, far above the Union armies. On the Union side Grant was mostly dealing with generals he did not know: Ambrose Burnside, Joseph Hooker, William F. Smith, and George H. Thomas. He was not sure how they would respond during a battle. Fortunately, on November 15, William T. Sherman arrived in Chattanooga.

The "Miracle at Missionary Ridge"

The battle began on November 25. Sherman attacked Missionary Ridge while Hooker struck Bragg's left **flank.** Soon both attacks stalled. Grant ordered Thomas's men to help Sherman. Suddenly, as Grant watched, the troops began marching straight up Missionary Ridge, an extremely dangerous operation. Confederates pounded them with fire, but they kept moving forward. Finally they reached the top, and Bragg's troops scattered.

African Americans and the Civil War

African-American soldiers served in Union **regiments** throughout the United States during the Civil War. On May 22, 1863, the Bureau of Colored Troops was established to expand the role of black units. About 200,000 men served in these regiments; and about 94,000 were former slaves in Confederate states. The remainder were freemen from the North or from border states. One of the best-known battles involving black troops occurred at Petersburg, Virginia, in July 1864. Union engineers dug a tunnel and placed dynamite beneath Confederate positions. After the dynamite exploded, Northern troops, led by black soldiers under Edward Ferrero, attacked. Many of them, however, fell into the crater produced by the explosion, and the result was a disaster. But the use of African-American troops helped convince Confederates that **slavery** was doomed.

This 1863 photograph shows General Ulysses S. Grant (left) and five other men on Lookout Mountain in Tennessee.

Grant was amazed at this success. In later years the Union charge would be known as the "Miracle of Missionary Ridge." Grant was so surprised he failed to pursue Bragg as he retreated. But the Battle of Chattanooga was over and the Union had again won a major victory. Grant's popularity in the North reached new heights.

10 General-in-Chief

1864

February
Grant named
lieutenant general

March 10
Grant visited Army
of the Potomac

May 4
Army of the
Potomac crossed
Rapidan River

May 8–20
Battle of
Spotsylvania

June 1–3
Battle of Cold
Harbor

November 4
Abraham Lincoln
reelected as
president

1865

April 9
Lee surrendered at
Appomattox

*O*nce again Grant turned his sights on Mobile. In the east, **Union** generals had made little progress against Robert E. Lee. In four major battles—Second Manassas, Fredericksburg, Chancellorsville, and Mine Run—Northern armies failed to advance against Lee. Lee had outlasted one general after another: Irwin McDowell, George McClellan, Ambrose Burnside, John Pope, and Joseph Hooker. By capturing Alabama, then Georgia, Grant thought he could slowly corner Lee and force him out of Virginia.

But again events moved in a different direction. In Washington, D.C. and around the country, Grant was mentioned as a possible presidential candidate. He rejected the idea right away: "I am not a candidate for any office nor for favors from any party. Let us succeed in crushing the rebellion, in the shortest possible time, and I will be content with whatever credit may then be given me . . ."

Lieutenant General

But to ensure Grant's support in the coming election, Lincoln and Congress promoted him to **lieutenant general.** This rank had rarely been awarded to American generals. Now Grant was general-in-chief of the entire Union army. He was responsible for all Northern forces and it would be up to him to win the war.

On March 8, 1864, he traveled to Washington, D.C., to receive his new title. Crowds mobbed him, trying to catch a glimpse of the "hero of Chattanooga." After the ceremony Grant visited the Army of the Potomac, which was responsible for defending Washington, D.C., and fighting

This photograph of George Gordon Meade was taken by Mathew Brady, a famous Civil War photographer.

George Gordon Meade

George Gordon Meade was born in Spain in 1815. He father was a wealthy merchant who was ruined during the Napoleonic Wars. Meade attended **West Point** and worked as an army engineer for many years, building lighthouses and coastal defenses. When the Civil War began, he led a group of Pennsylvania volunteers in major early battles against Robert E. Lee. On June 28, 1863, he was given command of the Army of the Potomac, whose other leaders had failed to make progress against Lee. He successfully drove Lee's forces out of Pennsylvania following the battle of Gettysburg, a turning point in the war. After the war ended, he remained in the army as a major general, before he died in 1872.

Robert E. Lee. The head of the army, George Meade, assumed Grant would take his place. But he was surprised when Grant expressed confidence in Meade and treated him as the commanding general.

Grant's strategy

At first Grant still planned to go back west and continue the fight there. But now he decided to remain in the east with the Army of the Potomac. While he fought Robert E. Lee, Sherman would take on Joseph E. Johnston, who had replaced

Bragg, and lead a charge into Georgia. Meanwhile, Nathaniel Banks would march on Mobile, and the Army of the James, under Benjamin F. Butler, would strike Richmond from the south, putting more pressure on Lee. This was Grant's strategy in the spring of 1864.

It took some work to win over the troops in the east. Some of them did not like that a westerner had been put in charge. He found the officers much harder to manage than those in his old army. Another difficulty was political. Grant considered several of the **Union** generals and officers **incompetent.** He wanted to remove them, but many had political connections. With a presidential election approaching in November, it was impossible to fire them.

The campaign in Virginia

Grant and Meade were ready to begin their attack on Lee's Army of Northern Virginia. On May 4, 1864, the Army of the Potomac crossed the Rapidan River. Soon Robert E. Lee brought his troops forward and attacked.

The two armies met in a woody, wild area known as the Wilderness. A month of almost continuous fighting followed. After the first three days brought many **casualties** but little success on either side, Grant left the Wilderness in the middle of the night. His troops swung south to Spotsylvania, where the battle resumed. The Union army caused heavy damage to Lee's men, but could not break through. The number of dead and wounded soldiers was rising higher. Grant wrote, "The world has never seen so bloody or protracted [long-lasting] a battle as the one being fought and I hope never will again."

Cold Harbor

Heavy rains at Spotsylvania kept the fighting to a minimum over the next several days. Grant decided to move once again to Lee's right, pushing deeper into Virginia. On June 1 the armies clashed at Cold Harbor. On June 3 the Union launched a major attack that failed miserably. Thousands of troops were mowed down from Lee's well-defended positions. By this time both sides were using more and more **trench**

warfare. Soldiers dug holes and trenches in the ground to defend themselves. It became difficult for Grant to make any forward progress.

Despite the setback, Grant remained confident. On June 12 he once again moved his army south. This time his destination was Petersburg, Virginia. This city controlled key railroad lines leading to Richmond. If Grant could conquer it, he would soon dominate the **Confederate** capital.

Siege at Petersburg

Grant's men successfully crossed the James River and reached Petersburg. But their first efforts to take the city failed. Grant prepared to lead another

This 1864 photograph shows General Grant with his staff at City Point, Virginia, which is where the Union troops made camp for the **siege** at Petersburg.

siege, similar to Vicksburg. This one, however, would last much longer. At Vicksburg Grant had surrounded Pemberton and cut him off from the outside world. But Lee still had supply lines bringing food and ammunition to his troops. Grant realized that to win he would have to destroy or capture the Weldon Railroad, which was used to bring supplies to Richmond.

By now there was so much arguing and fighting among Grant's own officers that he needed to reorganize his army. However, with the presidential election drawing closer, he still could not dismiss several politically connected generals. That led Grant to delay his final attack on Petersburg for some time. By August 1864 he was discouraged that he had not made better progress.

This photograph of General Ulysses S. Grant's staff was taken in City Point, Virginia, where the Union army set up camp for the siege of Petersburg.

Sherman's march to the sea

Meanwhile, Sherman, who had taken over the Army of Tennessee, had conquered Atlanta. He began marching his troops to the sea, destroying everything in his path. He hoped to break **Confederate** loyalty and encourage the South to rejoin the **Union.** Grant worried that in driving so far into Confederate territory, Sherman might not make it out. At the same time Philip Sheridan was winning victories in the Shenandoah Valley, increasing the pressure on Lee.

In November Lincoln was reelected. Now Grant could reorganize the army and prepare for a final blow against Petersburg. A wet winter and political distractions forced him to wait for spring. Finally, on March 31, 1865, the attack began. Philip Sheridan led a charge against Lee's right **flank.** By April 1 Sheridan had broken through and cut off Lee's supply lines. The following day the entire Union army rushed forward, only to find that Lee had retreated.

Victory at Appomattox

As Petersburg fell, the citizens and government at Richmond fled, too. The Union army captured both cities and pursued Lee to the west. By April 9 Lee was ready to surrender and he and Grant met at Appomattox Court House. Following Lincoln's orders, Grant was prepared to offer generous terms to end the war. He drew up a brief document indicating Lee's surrender. Grant wrote, "each officer and man will be allowed to return to their homes not to be disturbed by United States Authority . . ." He also allowed the Confederate soldiers to keep their private property, including their horses. Grant and Lincoln hoped in this manner to end the anger between the two sides as quickly as possible, so that the nation could again be one.

11 Reconstruction

1865

November
Grant toured
former
Confederate states

1867

Grant became
acting secretary
of war

1868

November
Grant elected
president

1872

November
Grant reelected
president

1884

Wall Street Panic
that cost Grant
his life savings

1885

Grant died in
Mt. McGregor,
New York

Five days after Lee's surrender, Abraham Lincoln was shot and killed. Andrew Johnson became president. Grant used his tremendous popularity to make sure Johnson continued Lincoln's policy of **reconciliation.** Johnson, for instance, wanted to try Robert E. Lee for **treason.** Grant threatened to **resign** until Johnson changed his mind.

In the fall of 1865, Grant toured the South. He decided that former **Confederates** had accepted the outcome of the war and that the two sides would quickly come together as one nation. As time passed, however, Grant began to doubt this judgment. As violence continued in the South against former slaves and government officials, he became critical of Johnson's policies. By 1868 he was ready to run for president as a **Republican.** He was easily elected, and then reelected in 1872.

Grant as president

Grant is often considered one of the worst presidents in American history. His administration was filled with **corrupt** and **incompetent** individuals. Some of them had served in his army staff or were family members. One **scandal** after another made it difficult for the president to accomplish much. His secretary of war, for instance, was **impeached** for selling government jobs. Grant was skilled when it came to judging human character during wartime, but in **civilian** life, he was easily deceived. Grant also made bad decisions, such as his failed plan to conquer the Dominican Republic.

Ulysses S. Grant gives his **inaugural address** at the United States Capitol on March 4, 1873.

But Grant's presidency included some important successes. He signed into law the Fifteenth Amendment, which banned racial **discrimination** in elections. He had to fight hard to make sure blacks could vote, especially in the South. Grant broke up the **Ku Klux Klan** and used federal troops to ensure fair elections. After he left office, however, blacks were often not allowed to vote in the South until the late 1960s.

Tourism, high finance, and writing

After deciding not to run for president again in 1876, Grant took a long two-year tour of the world. When he returned he ran for president a third time, but could

General Grant is seated, writing his memoirs at Mount McGregor, near Saratoga Springs, New York, on June 27, 1885.

not win the **Republican nomination.** He then invested most of his money in a Wall Street company. A financial panic in 1884 wiped out his entire savings, and left him $150,000 in debt. Even after all the changes in his life, he still was not a good businessman.

At almost the same time he learned that he had throat cancer. He knew that he would not live much longer. To make money for his family, and to pay off his debts, he began writing magazine articles about the Civil War. Many people were impressed with his writing ability. One of them was Mark Twain, the famous author of *The Adventures of Huckleberry Finn* and *The Adventures of Tom*

Sawyer, among other books. Twain offered to publish Grant's **memoirs,** and for the rest of his life Grant worked furiously to complete them. He often wrote while suffering intense pain. Finally the book was finished, and it was a tremendous success. It is often considered one of the best military memoirs ever written. His two volumes sold thousands of copies and rescued Grant from his financial problems. But days after finishing the book, Grant died.

Conclusion

Ulysses S. Grant had a remarkable life. By his late 30s, he had accomplished very little. Although he was a good soldier, he could not support his family in the style they expected, and he could not bear separation from them. He suffered bouts of alcoholism and was often depressed. He was not a good businessman either. But when the Civil War began, he climbed rapidly through the ranks, until eventually he commanded the entire **Union** army. He had many critics, some of whom believed he allowed too many young soldiers to die. But through persistence and daring, he was able to lead the Union to victory.

A huge crowd of people came out to watch Grant's funeral procession in New York on August 8, 1885. Grant's tomb is located in Morningside Heights in New York, overlooking the Hudson River.

Timeline

June 24, 1821	Jesse Grant and Hannah Simpson married in Ohio
April 27, 1822	Ulysses S. Grant born in Point Pleasant, Ohio
1823	Jesse Grant and family moved to Georgetown, Ohio
1836	Grant attended preparatory school in Maysville, Kentucky
1837	Jesse Grant elected mayor of Georgetown
1839–1843	Grant attended the U.S. Military Academy
September 1843	Grant reported to Jefferson Barracks near St. Louis, Missouri
April 1844	Grant and Julia Dent became engaged to be married
	Grant sent to Camp Salubrity in Louisiana
September 1845	Grant sent to Corpus Christi, Texas
May 8, 1846	First battle of Mexican War began
August 22, 1848	Grant and Julia Dent married in St. Louis
May 1850	Frederick, the Grants' first son, was born
July 5, 1852	Grant left New York for San Francisco, and then Fort Vancouver
January 5, 1854	Grant reassigned to Fort Humboldt, California
April 11, 1854	Grant **resigned** from the army
August 1855	Grant arrived back in St. Louis and began farming
Summer 1856	Hardscrabble was built
April 1860	Grant family arrived in Galena, Illinois, to take over family general store
November 1860	Abraham Lincoln elected president of the United States
December 1860– March 1861	Seven Southern states **seceded** from the **Union** and formed the **Confederate States of America**
March 13, 1861	American Civil War began at Fort Sumter
June 15, 1861	Grant named **colonel** of the Seventh District **Regiment**
August 1861	Grant promoted to **Brigadier General** of Volunteers
September 6, 1861	Grant's army took Paducah, Kentucky
November 7, 1861	Attack on Belmont, Missouri
February 5–15, 1862	Grant captured Forts Henry, Donelson, and Heiman
March 1862	Halleck given command in the west
April 6–7, 1862	Battle of Shiloh/Pittsburg Landing
May 1862	Beauregard evacuated Corinth
July 17, 1862	Grant took command of the District of West Tennessee
September 19, 1862	Price and Van Dorn attacked Corinth
December 29, 1862	Sherman defeated at Chickasaw Bayou
April 16, 1863	Porter's fleet sailed past Vicksburg
April 30, 1863	Grant crossed Mississippi River at Bruinsberg
May 14, 1863	Fall of Jackson, Mississippi

May 16, 1863	Battle of Champion Hill
July 4, 1863	Confederate surrender at Vicksburg
September 4, 1863	Grant thrown from his horse and injured
October 5, 1863	Halleck asked Grant to come to Chattanooga, Tennessee
October 27–28, 1863	Brown's ferry captured
November 15, 1863	Sherman arrived in Chattanooga
November 25, 1863	Battle of Chattanooga
February 1864	Grant named **lieutenant general**
March 10, 1864	Grant visited Army of the Potomac
May 4, 1864	Army of the Potomac crossed the Rapidan River
May 8–20, 1864	Battle of Spotsylvania
June 1–3, 1864	Battle of Cold Harbor
November 4, 1864	Abraham Lincoln reelected president
April 9, 1865	Robert E. Lee surrendered at Appomattox
November 1865	Grant toured the former Confederate states
1867	Grant became acting secretary of war
November 1868	Grant elected president of the United States
November 1872	Grant reelected president
1884	Wall Street Panic costed Grant his life savings
July 23, 1885	Grant died in Mount McGregor, New York

Further Reading

Brewer, Paul. *The American Civil War*. Chicago: Raintree, 1999.

Isaacs, Sally Senzell. *America in the Time of Abraham Lincoln (1815–1869)*. Chicago: Heinemann Library, 1999.

Naden, Corinne J., and Rose Blue. *Why Fight? The Causes of the American Civil War*. Chicago: Raintree, 2000.

Smolinski, Diane. *Key Battles of the Civil War*. Chicago: Heinemann Library, 2001.

Smolinski, Diane. *Soldiers of the Civil War*. Chicago: Heinemann Library, 2001.

Weber, Michael. *Civil War and Reconstruction*. Chicago: Raintree, 2000.

Glossary

abolitionist person who demanded that slavery be ended in the South

ambush surprise attack

arsenal building where weapons and military supplies are stored

boycott refuse to deal with a person, organization, or country, usually to show disapproval or to force acceptance of terms

brigadier general military officer who is one rank above a colonel

cadet student in a military academy

casualty military person lost during warfare

cavalry soldiers who ride horses

cholera dangerous infectious disease marked by vomiting and diarrhea

civilian person not on active duty in a military, police, or firefighting force

colonel army rank above lieutenant colonel and below brigadier general

Confederacy eleven Southern states that seceded from the United States between 1860 and 1861; a Confederate is a supporter, citizen, or soldier of the Confederacy

corrupt behaving in a bad or improper way; to change from good to bad

Democratic Party political organization formed by people who believed that government should be elected by the nation's people

discredit cause to seem dishonest or untrue

discrimination treating some people better than others without any fair or proper reason

elite group of people who have special advantages or privileges

flank far right or left end of an army's line of troops

garrison fort

humane having sympathy and consideration for others

impeach formally charge a public official with misconduct in office

incompetent not able to do a good job

infantry soldiers who walk, the main part of an army

Ku Klux Klan organization formed after Civil War to frighten African Americans and their supporters, restore white rule to the South, and prevent federal troops from occupying Southern areas

lieutenant general military rank below that of general

loyalist someone who remains loyal to a particular cause; during the American Civil War, a loyalist was someone who remained loyal to the Union

memoir story of a person's experiences and life

militia citizens banded together in a military unit

neutral not favoring either side in a fight, contest, or war

nomination act of choosing a candidate for election, appointment, or honor

petition document asking for something

plantation large farm on which crops are tended by laborers who also live there

quartermaster officer in charge of supplying and transporting troops

racist having a belief that a certain race or races are superior to others

reconciliation bringing two sides closer together after a fight or argument

recruit find new members; one of those new members is called a recruit

refugee person escaping suffering or oppression

regiment military unit

reinforcements troops sent to help a struggling army

Republican Party political organization formed by people opposed to slavery who felt that the United States government should not allow and abolish slavery in its new territories

resign quit or give up a job or other responsibility

secede separate from a larger unit, such as the Union; a person who supports seceding is called a secessionist

siege long assault on a town or fortress

slavery owning other human beings and forcing them to work

states' rights view that the laws and customs adopted by the individuals states, including slavery, should not be interfered with by the federal government.

sympathy readiness to favor or support; readiness to think or feel alike

tanner person who makes leather from animal hides

treason act of betrayal, such as against a country or government

trench warfare form of fighting in which troops dig holes in the earth to defend themselves

underestimate estimate as being less than the actual size, quantity, price, or number

Union another name for the United States of America; during the Civil War it referred to the states that remained loyal to the United States government

West Point United States Military Academy at West Point, New York; Grant and most of the major Civil War generals attended the school

Index

abolitionists 6, 14, 16
African Americans 31, 32, 41
American Anti-Slavery Society 6
Appomattox Court House 4, 39
Army of Northern Virginia 36
Army of Tennessee 39
Army of the James 36
Army of the Potomac 34–35, 36

Banks, Nathaniel P. 31, 36
Battle of Bull Run/Manassas 18, 25
Battle of Champion Hill 29–30, 30
Battle of Chancellorsville 34
Battle of Fredericksburg 34
Battle of Gettysburg 35
Battle of Mine Run 34
Battle of Missionary Ridge 32–33, 33
Battle of Monterey 11
Battle of Pittsburg Landing 22–23, 23
Battle of Second Manassas 34
Battle of Shiloh 22–23, 23
Battle of Vicksburg 27–28, 28
Battle of Wilson's Creek 18
Beauregard, Pierre 23, 24
Bowen, John S. 29
Bragg, Braxton 31, 32
Brown, John 16
Brown, William Wells 6
Buchanan, James 16
Buckner, Simon Bolivar 9
Buell, Don Carlos 23
Bureau of Colored Troops 32
Burnside, Ambrose 32, 34
Butler, Benjamin F. 36

Camp Salubrity 9
cholera 12
Civil War 18, 23, 28, 30, 33
Confederate States of America 4, 16, 17, 19,
    20, 22, 26, 29, 31, 39, 40
Cumberland River 20

Democratic Party 16
Dent, Frederick 9
Dent, Julia. See Grant, Julia Dent.
discrimination 41
Douglass, Frederick 6

Emancipation Proclamation 29, 31

Ferrero, Edward 32
Fifteenth Amendment 41
Foote, Andrew H. 21
Forrest, Nathan Bedford 26
Fort Donelson 20–21, 22
Fort Heiman 20–21
Fort Henry 20–21, 22
Fort Humboldt 13
Fort Sumter 16
Fort Vancouver 13
Fourth Infantry 9

Garrison, William Lloyd 6
Grant, Frederick Dent (son) 12
Grant, Hanna Simpson (mother) 6, 7
Grant, Jesse Root (father) 6, 7
Grant, Julia Dent (wife) 9–10, 10, 12, 13,
    14, 15, 19
Grant, Simpson (uncle) 15
Grant, Ulysses, Jr. (son) 14
Grant, Ulysses S. 5, 42
    alcohol and 13, 21, 22, 31, 43
    at Fort Humboldt 13
    battles 19, 21, 22–23, 26–27, 29–30, 30
    birth of 6, 7
    as brigadier general 18
    at Camp Salubrity 9
    childhood of 7
    as colonel of Seventh District Regiment 17
    death of 43
    education of 7–9
    as farmer 14–15
    at Fort Vancouver 13
    horses and, 7, 8, 31
    at Jefferson Barracks 9
    as lieutenant general 34
    as major general 21, 30
    marriage of 12
    memoirs of 5, 43
    paintings by 8
    as president 5, 40–41, 41
    as quartermaster 10
    as real estate partner 15
    as recruiter 17, 31
    resignation of 13
    world tour 41
    as writer 42–43
Grierson, Benjamin 28

Halleck, Henry 20, 21, 22, 24, 31
Hardscrabble cabin 14, 15
Harper's Ferry, Virginia 16
Hooker, Joseph 32, 34

Ingalls, Rufus 9

Jackson, Thomas J. 9
Jefferson Barracks 9
Johnson, Andrew 40
Johnston, Joseph E. 29, 35–36
Johnston, Sidney 22

Ku Klux Klan 41

Lee, Robert E. 4, 16, 26, 34, 40
Lincoln, Abraham 16, 24, 29, 34, 39, 40

maps 8, 19
McClellan, George B. 9, 34
McClernand, John A. 26
McDowell, Irwin 34
McPherson, James 29
Meade, George Gordon 35, 36
Mexican War 4, 10–11, 11, 20
Missouri 17–18

Nelson, William 23

Panama 12
Parker, Theodore 6
Pemberton, John C. 26, 27, 30
Pillow, Gideon 20
Polk, James K. 10
Polk, Leonidas 20
Pope, John 34
Porter, David D. 28
Prentiss, Benjamin 22, 23
Price, Sterling 26

quartermasters 10, 11, 12

racism 4, 25
Rawlins, John A. 16
refugees 25
Republican Party 16
Rosecrans, William 31

Scott, Winfield 10
secession 4, 16, 18, 24
Seventh District Regiment 17
Sheridan, Philip 39
Sherman, William T. 9, 22, 24, 25, 26, 32,
    35, 39
Siege of Petersburg 37–38
slavery 4, 6, 10, 14, 16, 25
Smith, William E. 32
states' rights 4
Stowe, Harriet Beecher 6

Taylor, Zachary 10
Tennessee River 20
Thomas, George H. 9, 32
trench warfare 36–37
Twain, Mark 5, 42–43
Twenty-First Illinois Volunteers 17, 18

Uncle Tom's Cabin (Harriet Beecher
    Stowe) 6
Underground Railroad 6
Union 4, 16, 24, 26, 32, 36, 39, 43
United States Military Academy. See West
    Point.

Van Dorn, Earl 26

Webster, Joseph 23
Weld, Theodore Dwight 6
West Point military academy 7, 8, 20, 25, 35
White Haven plantation 9, 14
Wilderness 36

Yates, Richard 17